Jacob's Revelation

Robin Reimers

Copyright © 2025 by ROBIN REIMERS

All rights reserved. No part of this publication may be reproduced, distributed or transmitted in any form or by any means, including photocopying, recording, or other electronic or mechanical methods, without the prior written permission of the publisher, except in the case of brief quotations embodied in critical reviews and certain other noncommercial uses permitted by copyright law. For permission requests, write to the publisher, addressed "Attention: Permissions Coordinator," at the address below.

ROBIN REIMERS /Author's Tranquility Press
2300 Camp Creek Parkway Ste 120 #1255
College Park, GA 30337
www.authorstranquilitypress.com

Ordering Information:
Quantity sales. Special discounts are available on quantity purchases by corporations, associations, and others. For details, contact the "Special Sales Department" at the address

CONTENTS

Preface iv

   Chapter 1: **The Gift** 1

   Chapter 2: **Love and War** 3

   Chapter 3: **Confusion** 5

   Chapter 4: **My Parents** 8

   Chapter 5: **The Revelation** 29

   Chapter 6: **Mending Hearts** 31

   Chapter 7: **My Father's Last Days** 33

   Chapter 8: **Open Your Heart** 37

PREFACE

My purpose in writing this book is to give comfort and strength to families, and hope and faith to the dying.

I started to believe in Yeshua when I was twenty-one years old in Israel. I had always loved God and wanted to know him better. Before I was twenty-one, I resented Yeshua because I thought all Christians hated the Jews because they believed we killed Jesus. I did not realize it was God's will, that if he did not die, we could not accept him as our Savior, and we would not have eternal life. "His blood makes atonement for our sins." (Leviticus 17:11)

When I accepted Yeshua, my parents thought I was confused and took me to deprogrammers. My father would not step foot in a church and always told me how he didn't believe in God—and that he wouldn't unless he saw for himself. Their attempts to stop me from believing did not work; God rescued me.

Many years after I accepted Yeshua, my father, a Jewish man (Priest of Levi) of almost ninety years old, who had little faith, wound up in a wheelchair.

Then, a miracle happened—a miracle that could not be explained in any other way than … by the hand of God! My father saw Yeshua for himself, and it was on that day that he realized Yeshua was real. It was on that day that he got out of his wheelchair and claimed to all that Yeshua was, is, and always will be the savior of the world!

This book is written to show all that Jesus is the truth.

I want to thank my daughter Rachel for helping with the description of my book, my son Michael for the title "Jacob's Revelation," my husband Glenn for the outer covering, my friends Marcia and Frank for helping with scriptures, my friend Gail for the encouragement to write this book, my friend Sandra for her dream and caring. Most of all, to Yeshua, for without him there would be no need for writing this book. The author is Yeshua.

Chapter 1:

The Gift

The month of April is said to be a time when nature shows its most beloved creations. Nature shows her majestic trees swaying in a way that makes your eyes stare in awe. She shows her flowers, brighter than even the sun itself. But most of all, April was the month God gave Jacob Aaron Schoenes to the world.

This man, born in Brooklyn, New York, in 1918, was a man of unsurpassable love and joy. But before we dive into how this man turned out to be such a wonderful person and what made him the bold and beautiful man that he finally turned out to be, let us look at his roots.

This where we find out about his parents. Both Russians were in love with their professions and each other. His father was one of the greatest electricians of his time. A man to be looked up to and admired. And his son— my father—did just that. My father's life changed when his father died. My father was younger than the age of thirteen. As a Jewish boy during the Great Depression, he had to take care of his family or face being thrown out into the streets, without any money. With the burden of taking care of and providing for his family on his shoulders, my father had his Bar Mitzvah to symbolize how he was now a man and had the responsibility to hold his family up as one. My father was not the only hard worker in his family. His mother inspired him. She worked as a dressmaker, for long hours for a small salary, and still managed to provide food for the family. In fact, she was such a great cook that my father, decades later, still described the taste and enjoyment of eating her food. His mother gave him the greatest gift, memories of her love and dedication to her family. This love and dedication would help my father turn into the man he became.

Chapter 2:

Love and War

Jacob was a man in love with his country, so in love that he enlisted to serve in World War II and was eventually promoted to sergeant. He served his country in Egypt, and it almost cost him his life.

Without God, my father would have lost his life. Submarines during the war were dangerous. Although there were minefields and enemies at every foot, my father still took the risk of taking control of a ship. On that mission, he was one breath away from a life-taking mine. God saved him by showing another ship the mine and they soon radioed my father to warn him about it. God had more in store for my father!

My father married his first wife before the war. Soon my two older sisters were born—Lorraine and then Michele, two opposites. The only time my father was ever mad during this time of his life was when my oldest sister was born while he was still overseas. For some reason, he was denied his leave and it caused him to go into a depression. His depression got worse just after World War II when his first wife died of breast cancer. He lost all faith in

God for many years until he came back to the Lord at eighty-seven years old! This is when Yeshua came to him. Before this encounter, my father did not trust in God but in man. The Lord tells us to "trust in the Lord and let him guide you." (Proverbs 3:5–7)

Now let's get back to when his wife died. You see, though he experienced depression, this man's heart did not break after his first marriage. "His love never dies." Six months after his first wife died, he met my mother and remarried. God always gives us what we desire. We might not get it when we want it, but God—in his own timing—tends to give us our heart's desire when we need it most. After all, God's work shines brightest when you cannot see a way out. So, God gave my mother to my father, and soon he gave both of them to me.

Chapter 3:

Confusion

My father worked hard as a bus driver and mechanic when I was growing up in New York. Our family lived in a two-family home in Brooklyn until we moved to Florida when I was sixteen years old. He worked all the time: we never went to the temple, never prayed, and never read God's word! My parents never taught us about God, even though my mom's grandfather was a "Rabbi." My parents were proud of their heritage, but they knew nothing about the love of this God they always heard about. It was sad but true.

At the age of twenty-one, I went to Israel on a Kibbutz. It was there that my relationship with Yeshua started. When I came home, my parents thought I was confused and sent me to many rabbis, hoping they could succeed in deprogramming me. However, what the Rabbis did not know was that my faith in God was strong. They asked me many hard-to-answer questions. I could not quote the Bible when trying to answer since I was a new believer and not yet wholly familiar with the scriptures.

The Rabbis finally said, "How could you believe in something that you don't know anything about?"

I simply said, "How could I not believe in something that has brought me closer than I have ever been in my life to my one and only savior?" The power of God overwhelmed them leaving them speechless as I left the room filled with a passion for my newfound savior.

I grew up as well and have two children. Their father is a Muslim and he explained his faith to me. In an attempt to share the love of God, I asked him some questions. One of them stumped him completely: "Where would you go if you died today?" I said.

"I would go to heaven with many virgins serving me day and night as a reward for my life," he answered.

"I, being female, would not like female virgins serving me. I would prefer male bodybuilders," I said.

"I do not know about that," he said.

"Where is God in this?" I asked. "How are you worshipping God if your eyes are only on the virgins? God is a jealous God and does not like to share his attention."

After ten years, my first husband and I parted with our different beliefs. But this story is not about my relationship with my past husband. This story is about my father, a man who likewise stood steadfast in his beliefs, and changed when the love of Yeshua was revealed to him. It is about "Jacob's revelation." But before I get into that, you must know about both my mother and father.

Chapter 4:

My Parents

My mother and father lived in a condo in Tamarac, Florida, for over thirty years. I missed them terribly even though I lived only half an hour away in Coral Springs. We visited them frequently, and my children loved them dearly. Many times, we would try to share the love of Yeshua, but my dad just would not listen. Thankfully my mother eventually came to hear about the Lord when I witnessed her on the phone without my father knowing about it. Soon, she came to accept him in her heart as Lord and Savior.

In Isaiah 53, God talks about how the Messiah will be "rejected of his own people," but that was God's will because only with a pure sacrifice could our sins be washed away forever. "By his stripes (how he was whipped by Roman soldiers) we are healed!" I also explained to my mother how in Micah 5:2 God talks about how the Messiah will come out of Bethlehem, and his name will be Emmanuel. (God with us.)

The love of God gave my mother strength. One day, my mother called me and said she could not walk because her legs hurt so much. She was going to call 911. I rushed over to her house with my children and I asked her if I could pray for her in the name of Yeshua, as He is the God who heals. I told her the verse that proclaims how the stripes Yeshua endured for us give us the power to receive healing and asked her if she believed that. She said, "Yes." I told her to thank him for his healing and get up and walk. Amazingly, she did! She was thanking the Lord and walking. All the pain in her legs left her body when she started to believe in Yeshua.

My mother then was diagnosed with cancer. I was oblivious to the fact that my mother was dying; my father kept the diagnosis to himself in order not to upset me.

A few months later, my mother was hospitalized, and the nurses in the hospital stated that my mother had taken a turn for the worse. I felt in my heart the need to ask my father to come to church on Easter Sunday and pray with me. He actually came, and after the service that day, my mother was better. A few days later, she was discharged from the hospital and went home.

Truly, by his stripes, we are healed. God soon took my mother in his own time. The day she died was a terrible day, but everything happens for a reason, and God always cares about his children, no matter what we think.

After my mother died, my father grew ill and soon became crippled in a wheelchair. He was one of those people who believed the mind controls all matters of the body; he believed his mind would help him overcome the illness he was suffering from.

Knowing God is the most powerful doctor of all, I told my father that if his mind did not heal him, he should see if Yeshua would. It was then that my father decided to come to church with my family. That day is a day I will never forget. When I found out he would be coming that next Sunday, I talked to him about Yeshua and Acts 2:38, when Peter says that we all must "repent and be baptized, every one of you, in the name of Jesus Christ, for the remission of sins and you shall receive the gift of the Holy Ghost." My father was touched when I told him that Yeshua was knocking at the door of his heart and that all my father had to do was open it for Him to step through. God soon touched my father's heart, and he repented of his sins and accepted Yeshua to come into his heart.

My father in World War 2.

My Dad early years with my sister Lorraine.

My parents and I.

My parents.

Christmas time with my Dad, me and my 2 children.

My Dad after he saw Jesus, you can see glow on him.

My Dad and my sister Michele reunited after 20 years after Jesus changed him.

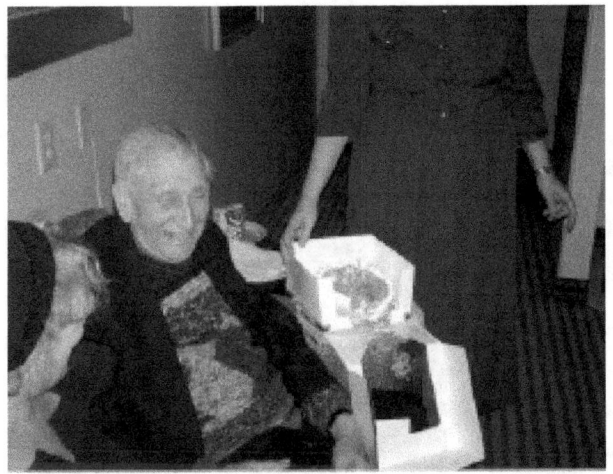

Chapter 5:

The Revelation

That day that my father went to church with us, a miracle happened. Since his mind had not been able to heal him, my father went to church and prayed to get out of his wheelchair. He stood up in the middle of service! The next service he had a walker, and the next one, a cane. Finally, he did not need any aid at all! Praise God!

I asked my father if would he like to use a cane, just to be safe. He replied, "Yeshua healed me, that is all I need." From that time on, he believed in Yeshua. I didn't realize how awesome my father's encounter with God was until two years later.

My father once told me that his grandmother said he was a descendant of the tribe of Levi. He did not know what the tribe was in the time of Moses, so he asked me since I knew about the Bible. I told him it meant he was a priest of God. Thousands of years ago, on the day of Yom Kippur, only the priest of Levi could enter the holy of holies, where the Ark of the Covenant was, and ask God for forgiveness for the Jewish people. I suddenly realized why Yeshua had come to my dad so fervently. It was because our family's lineage originated from the people who had the most direct connection to Him in the ancient days.

I noticed a difference in my father before and after he was saved. Before he repented of his sins, he was selfish and hardly thought of others. He would not let my mother go to church. He did not speak to my sister Michele for twenty years. He had a heart filled with anger instead of forgiveness. He never went to the temple, never read the Bible, and never prayed. We never had a real Passover; our Passover was going to a restaurant to eat a regular dinner! Then my father was saved; he repented of his sins, and he accepted Yeshua as his Lord and Savior and received the Holy Ghost.

After that, there were many changes in his life. He cared for people and prayed for people. I even saw God use my father in miraculous ways. When my father prayed, people with walkers and canes started to walk. God anointed his heart, and my father shared the love of God each and every day with anyone who would listen. He even went to a Hassidic temple where he prayed and told them his story about Yeshua, and they listened to him.

Chapter 6:

Mending Hearts

My father and my sister hadn't spoken in twenty years due to their bitterness toward each other. It touched my heart when my father made up with my sister after this long period. There was a big change in my father's life thanks to God. I saw how he loved people and how God changed his heart and spirit.

One day, on Yom Kippur, we were in the temple and my father told the Rabbi and his wife the most fantastic story! He told them how two years before, when he was in church, all the people disappeared and a man dressed in a white robe with a red sash wrapped around his waist came to him, took his hand, and called him by name. The man said, "Jack, get up out of that wheelchair! You do not belong there!" When my father took the man's hand, he looked at his wrist and saw a scar. My father asked the mysterious man "What is that?" And the man said, "That is where I was crucified." Curiosity took over, so my dad asked the mysterious man a question: "Who are you?" The man said, "I am Yeshua, (Jesus), the God who heals you."

When Rabbi Lash from Lauderhill, Florida, heard this story, he had my father witness to everyone in the temple. Seeing the people's faces is something I will never forget. It was as though their lives, their stress, all were washed away. It was as if when the name "Jesus" is spoken, all fall to the floor with passion and the truest love. It is the kind of love that makes your heart beat wildly when you are with your love and the love that makes your heart freeze when he leaves.

It was on this day that all who heard my father's story understood the true love of God. God is my entire world, my entire life. Likewise, God loves each and every one of us unconditionally. It is a love greater than any other you will ever feel in this world. This love is all I need and all I will ever want. It is sufficient. My father felt the same way I did ever since he saw Yeshua in the church and God healed him from the wheelchair.

I asked my father why he had never told me the story before—for almost two years. I knew he was healed in the church when he got out of the wheelchair, but I had no idea that he saw Yeshua. He then told me that he could not say anything till the right time, in the temple. Yeshua wanted to wait until the right time to reveal this miracle.

Chapter 7:

My Father's Last Days

My father lived till his ninetieth birthday, and a few weeks later, the Lord took him. He was eighty-seven when he first received the Lord, showing that God could use anyone at any age. It is never too late to come to Jesus.

During his last year, my father suffered from heart failure. He was in and out of the hospital on several occasions. He became very weak, so I asked the doctor to put him in hospice.

For two days while he was in a coma, I was always by his side holding his hand. I kept praying to God to take him and even told my father it was okay to go. For two long days, nothing happened! Why did God not answer me? I held my father's hand and kept saying, "I love you, Daddy, if you hear me, squeeze my hand—even a little—so I know you are listening." Nothing happened! His hand was frozen, did not move an inch ... I prayed and prayed. I did not want to see my father suffer any longer. I wanted Jesus to take him. Why didn't he hear my prayer?

Then, to my surprise, my friend Sandra called me on the phone from Ohio and said that my father had come to her in a dream and told her that he was going to heaven and he felt no pain. He told her that he knew I loved him. I remembered holding his hand and telling him I loved him many times; I did not think he heard me but he did! Last but not least, through the dream, he told me my mother was coming to meet him that day and together they were going to heaven to meet the Lord Jesus in the air. I asked my friend, Sandra, "Today?" She said, "Yes, today."

As soon as Sandra finished talking to me on the phone, my father took his last breath and died within minutes. It seems as though he wanted me to have this message before he died.

During the last few minutes of his life, my husband, who never saw anything supernatural and always questioned supernatural experiences, had his own encounter. He said that minutes before my father died the room changed from color to black and white, and he actually saw my father's spirit leave his body and go up to heaven. That encounter gave him more faith in God. After my father's death, I felt peace because he did not suffer.

My father had talked about how he longed to see my mother and go to heaven with her. He did not know that I had witnessed to my mother a few years before on the phone and she had accepted

Yeshua as her Lord and Savior, after her own healing experience. She is with my father now; they are in heaven together.

During my father's funeral, it was a happy time because he was going home to meet the Lord, and I am sure the Lord is using him mightily in heaven.

When he died, there was another miracle; all his age left him. He looked like thirty years old again and had no wrinkles. He wore the Yamika and the prayer shawl. I put the Bible by his heart so he would always have the Lord there with him. I did the same thing for my mother.

I know my father is happy now together with my mother.

I know with prayer God gave me the strength to overcome, and the peace to go through the passing of my mother and my father within four years of each other.

I know how God gave me peace. With faith and prayer, God can do anything for anyone who asks.

Ask and you shall receive!

Chapter 8:

Open Your Heart

There is more to life than what we realize. In this world, we are only passing through. Our real home is with the Lord. You must be born again and filled with God's spirit to see him. I am a witness to this, along with my husband, my two children, two Rabbis and their congregation in Lauderhill and Coral Springs, Hassidic Jews who went to my father's gravesite and prayed for him, and the members of the Pentecostals of Cooper City, Florida, with Pastor Hattabaugh.

All these people have heard my father's testimony. I hoped he would have been able to continue to tell the world, but I will now continue my father's legacy—the priest of Levi's testimony—wherever I can. Now his legacy is passed on to my son Michael.

My purpose is to comfort families and the dying, to assure them that there is no pain in death, only joy if you know Yeshua. I hope this book helps you realize that there is life after death.

Those who humble themselves and surrender their life and will over to the Father by the way of Yeshua, the Messiah, and receive His atonement for sins, will inherit eternal life in His kingdom, the glorious kingdom of God. We can't do it on our own. Even all of our best works fall short of the glory of God. We can't try to live well on our own, because the devil and sin are real, trying to manipulate and deceive our thoughts and lives. Hell is real. The Lord said our best works are as filthy rags in the sight of God. Heaven is a free gift; it is not earned or deserved. His blood makes atonement for our sins (Leviticus 17:11).

If you want Yeshua as Lord of your life, repeat these words:

Yeshua, (Jesus) I am a sinner, I repent of my sins. I believe you. I believe you are my Lord and Savior. Come into my heart and change me to be the type of person you want me to be. Amen.

If you have done this, ask Yeshua to lead you to a Bible-believing church with believers who teach the book of Acts and believe the message of salvation. Believe, repent of your sins, be baptized in Jesus' name, and then you will receive the Holy Spirit (Acts 2:38), like my father, evidenced by the ability to speak in tongues. You shall then live a better life the way God wants you to live. Then, whenever the Lord takes you home, you will be prepared to meet him face to face. You will also be reunited with your loved ones who also believed the truth that set them free.

Congratulations on your new life and the peace that God gives you when you put your life in his hands.

Trust in the Lord and let Him guide you. (Proverbs 3:5–7)

May God bless you with strength and faith in Him. I hope this book has been a blessing to your life. If it has, please e-mail me, at robinlaurie7@gmail.com I would love to know.

www.ingramcontent.com/pod-product-compliance
Lightning Source LLC
LaVergne TN
LVHW020445080526
838202LV00055B/5349